Guess Whose Shadow?

Stephen R. Swinburne

Boyds Mills Press

Foreword

When the sun shines, you can see a world full of shadows. Look around, the shadows are everywhere. Cats have one and chairs have one. Flags, ice cream cones, and snowmen have them, too. Even clouds and airplanes have shadows.

Shadows come in every shape and size. Ants have small shadows while elephant shadows are huge. But sometimes a small object can have a very big shadow if the sun is low in the sky. Shadows are fat, thin, short, tall, round, square. They can be as still as a building or as fast as a basketball game.

What makes a shadow? Three things make a shadow: a light, an object, and a surface. For example, if sunlight shines on an object such as a bee, a shadow is made on the surface behind the bee. The bee's body blocks out the sunlight and makes a shadow.

The biggest shadow on earth is called night. Night is made when the sun shines on one side of the earth while the other side is cast in shadow. Inside your house at night, shadows are made from the light of lamps and flashlights. If you hold your hands between a light and the wall, you can have fun making hand shadows.

Shadows are always with you as you move through a sunny day. They keep you company. Shadows are a beautiful part of our everyday lives. When you step outside on the next sunny day, watch the shadows come and go.

—Steve Swinburne

Shadows are everywhere.

Once you know they are there,
you can find lots of them.

You have a shadow, too.
Your shadow follows you wherever you go.

Your shadow can be in front of you.

Your shadow can be
behind you, below you, or next to you.

But it is always there.

Your shadow appears when sunshine
or other light falls on you.

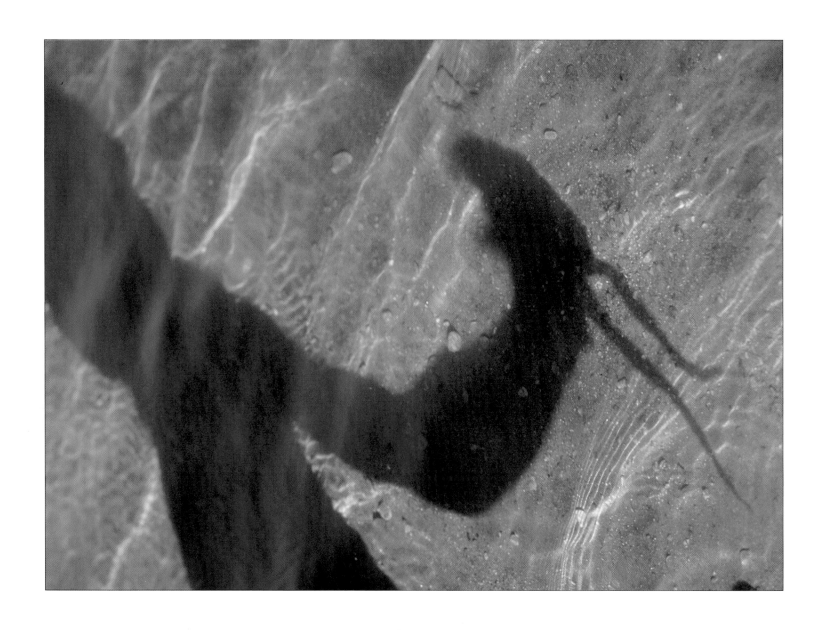

The shaded or dark area behind you is called a shadow.

If the sun is shining, anything will have a shadow.

Some shadows are big.

Some shadows are small.

You can play a game with shadows.

You can go on a shadow hunt.
Can you guess whose shadow?

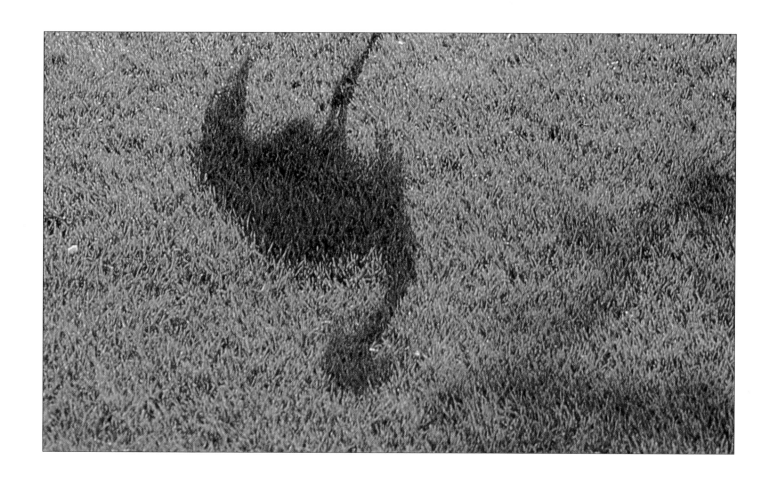

Guess whose shadow?

Guess whose shadow?

Guess whose shadow?

Guess whose shadow?

Guess whose shadow?

Guess whose shadow?

Some days, it's cloudy,
and you can't find your shadow.

But soon the sun shines,
and your shadow is right by your side.

Shadows make great sunny day friends.

To Mom and Lou, with all my love
—S. R. S.

Acknowledgements

Many thanks to the children of the Northwest Elementary School in Rutland, Vermont, and the kids
at the West River Farmer's Market in Londonderry, Vermont. Special thanks to Mark Lee, Nick Romolo, Sebby Spassoff, Devon and
Hayley Swinburne, and their awesome shadows.

Boyds Mills Press, Inc.
A Highlights Company
815 Church Street
Honesdale, Pennsylvania 18431
Printed in China

Publisher Cataloging-in-Publication Data

Swinburne, Stephen R.
Guess whose shadow? / by Stephen Swinburne.—1st ed.
[32]p. : col. ill. ; cm.
Summary: A photo-essay on how light creates shadows.
ISBN 1-56397-724-9 Hardcover
ISBN 1-59078-017-5 Paperback
1. Shadows—Juvenile literature. 2. Photography—Juvenile literature.
[1. Shadows. 2. Photography.] I. Title.
770 —dc21 [E] 1999 AC CIP
Library of Congress Catalog Card Number 98-072492

First Boyds Mills Press paperback edition, 2002
Book designed by Stephen R. Swinburne.
The text of this book is set in 24-point Garamond.

10 9 8 7 6 5 4   Hardcover
10 9 8 7 6 5 4 3 2   Paperback